# Now What?

"How to succeed even if college is not an option for you."

*by* **Kevin Ray Johnson**

• Chicago •

# Now What?

"How to succeed even if college is not an option for you."

*by* Kevin Ray Johnson

*Published by*
**Joshua Tree Publishing**
**• Chicago •**
JoshuaTreePublishing.com

All rights reserved. No part of this book may be reproduced or transmitted in any form or by any means, electronic or mechanical, including information storage and retrieval system without written permission from the publisher, except by a reviewer who may quote brief passages in a review.

13-Digit ISBN: 978-1-941049-05-1
Copyright 2020. Kevin Ray Johnson. All rights reserved.
Cover Image: Copyright © 2020 Tatiana Shepeleva

**Disclaimer:**
This book is designed to provide information about the subject matter covered. The opinions and information expressed in this book are those of the author, not the publisher. Every effort has been made to make this book as complete and as accurate as possible. However, there may be mistakes both typographical and in content. Therefore, this text should be used only as a general guide and not as the ultimate source of information. The author and publisher of this book shall have neither liability nor responsibility to any person or entity with respect to any loss or damage caused or alleged to be caused directly or indirectly by the information contained in this book.

Printed in the United States of America

# Table of Contents

| | |
|---|---|
| Introduction | 5 |
| Motivation and Discipline | 9 |
| Famous People without a College Degree | 13 |
| High School | 15 |
| Technical and Vocational Schools | 19 |
| Certifications | 21 |
| Volunteer | 23 |
| Self-Employed | 27 |
| Trades | 29 |
| Résumé Writing | 35 |
| Job Search | 39 |
| Finding a Job through Adversities | 43 |
| Interview Ready | 47 |
| Confidence | 53 |
| Conclusion | 55 |
| About the Author | 57 |
| Acknowledgments | 59 |

# Introduction

Congrats on graduating high school! The open house was wonderful, and hey, you made a few bucks. Now what? What do you do now? Where do you go? How do you get there? How do you get there without a college degree? Nobody is hiring. Nobody cares. You're not ready. It seems too hard. Your friends aren't going to college. You never thought about these things.

Right now is the most valuable time in your life. You just need to know that this is a gift, and you will succeed. Take a deep breath and take a moment to think about the future. I mean, why not just finish three years of high school? You're tired, right? And everyone is asking, "So now what?" What are you going to do now? You fire off something just to get them off your back and stop asking that question. The problem is that the answer you just gave them is what they want to hear, not what you want to do.

Nobody understands what you are thinking right now. No one knows what you have been through—the heartaches, the tough situations, the lack of guidance, and the feeling of not being loved. You have many other obstacles, such as having no money, no help, no support, and no hope. Do me a favor right now. Look at the very back of this book, and then come back here. This guy cares. This guy believes in you. This guy has been there. This guy knows you can do it. Now at this point, you are probably wondering why I'm holding a chicken. Well, it is because when you graduate, you have so many people pulling on you, such as your family, friends, and schools, asking, "What now?" You are just like a chicken running around with its head cut off. We are going to fix all of that, and it starts now. I want you to remember this for me: fear is a liar.

I understand. I know it is hard, and I know you feel alone right now. I was a middle child. I often felt that when my older brother was born, my parents were like, "Oh, look, a beautiful boy." But when I was born, they looked at me and said, "Hey, this isn't a girl. Get out of the way." My father left us when I was five years old. He had four little kids and a wife. My mother's boyfriends were no picnic either. I got a stepdad who did provide for us until I was seventeen. Then my mother left him.

We were living in a small, old rundown house in New Chicago, Indiana, and yes, we were those poor hillbilly people. I was once told we were swamp rats. By the way, that's not nice. I went to Portage High School, and my senior year was supposed to be the best. I was going to be a starting receiver for the football team and a track phenom. It was then my mother decided that it was time for her to live her life and basically threw us all out. I had an older brother and two little sisters, and we were now homeless for the most part.

I moved to West Virginia and lived with my family during my senior year. I then moved out with one month of school left to graduate because of conflicts. I lived in a park under a gazebo. I slept on a picnic table for three weeks. I walked to school early every morning so I could shower. I only ate half my lunch so I could bring the other half back in my pocket to eat for dinner. If this isn't enough negativity and pain to make a kid snap, I don't know what is, my friend. I had everything I needed to be a bad person. This was the crossroads, and I was right here staring at it. The sadness, pain, fear, and loneliness were more than I could handle. Just when I thought I was going down, something changed my life forever.

I remember lying there on this picnic table in the dark, staring up at the stars, wondering why I was put on this earth and what my purpose was. Obviously, nobody cared, so why should it matter, anyway? Heck, there wasn't anyone who could even stop me now. Lying there at that exact moment, I was thinking about all the terrible things in my life. Then I realized something—I had a choice. I was at the crossroads, and I had a choice to make right here, right now. Should

I take the left road and become an evil person with a criminal life that revolved around drugs, prison, and sadness (perhaps even worse, I'd end up dead), or should I take the right road? The right road was discipline, determination, guts, pride, and a willingness to conquer all obstacles that would get in my way.

I am strong, just like you are right here, right now. You know how I know this? It's because you're reading this book right now. My eyes were filled with tears of joy at that moment when I decided I would never quit, never give in ever again. I even said a prayer, and you know what? The very next day, one of my teachers who had been watching me falling apart, offered his trailer so I would have a place to stay—and I took it.

Help will come to you in the strangest ways, but you have to recognize it when you see it. This teacher provided me with a room, clothes, food, and a key to his trailer. What I'm trying to say is that you must want it for yourself. You have to have the guts to want to be better than you are today. Then go get it. This isn't about your mom or dad or even about your brothers and sisters. This is about what you want, period. I once heard a motivational speaker say, "If life knocks you down, try to land on your back because if you can look up, you can get up." Your parents fed you. The school taught you. Now, go get what's yours.

# Motivation and Discipline

This is where you might think I'm going to tell you to stop what you're doing and put that Xbox down, right? That you need to listen to your mom and dad and get off that phone. That you won't be anything if you don't start doing something now. Sound familiar?

What I will tell you is that none of us are the same. We all have different ideas, dreams, and needs. I don't know what your home life was like, and I don't know what you want to be in the future. What I do know is that you are now an adult. You are the master of your future. Do you remember when you were a little kid and you dreamed of being a police officer or an architect or even the president of the country? It is a scary thought when you recognize that your future starts right now, but you just have to turn that fear into motivation. Turn confusion into discipline. Take the first step toward your future.

You know, I found out later in life that if I had only told people I was mapping out a plan for my future and that they had to give me a minute to set a course, they most likely would have given me space. It's when we keep it all in and not tell them what we are doing that they panic. Don't be afraid to tell them that you are planning your future and that you got this. Don't be afraid to tell them to chill and that you will figure it out.

You need to realize that, at this point in your life, your parents and your school have done all they can do to get you ready for your own life. The good and bad things that you have experienced have made you tough. The mere fact that you survived to this point tells us that you are a survivor and you really can do anything you want. The question is, are you going to carry all that excess baggage with you? Can you accept things that happened? Can you not allow anything to take your future away from you? After you turn eighteen, you decide what is best for you. Anything that gets in your way is an obstacle. The cool thing is that you are now old enough to get rid of it. Well, you might want to wait until you get your own place before you hand out "no thank you" cards. You kind of need your parents for a little while longer.

The bottom line is that many things can squash your dreams, like carrying the past with you, confusion, fear, and things like drugs and alcohol. Again, anything that tries to get in your way is an obstacle.

You need to know that not all of this is your fault. How can people expect you to reach for the stars when they haven't shown you how to do it? Don't get me wrong. The school did give you the education and your parents gave you shelter, food, and financial assistance. I'm just saying it would have been nice if someone would have shown you how to do this rather than tell you, "Go get a job and do it right now." That's okay. Let's do this together. I'm right here. You can do it.

The one thing I (or anyone else for that matter) can't instill in you is the willingness to succeed. I know you've heard it a million times, but you are the only one who can stand up and take these steps.

# Famous People without a College Degree

Understand that I'm not telling you not to go to college. I'm simply showing you that you don't have to go to college to be somebody. Many parents dream of their kid going off to school and becoming a professional specializing in something. The reality is that many choose not to go to college at all but still have a rewarding, memorable life and job. College isn't for everyone. Just the thought of owing $50,000 to $150,000 on a student loan is nuts.

According to the Washington Post (source: US Bureau of the Census, June 26, 2018), only 27% of college graduates have a job related to their major. The study found that more than 40% of college graduates take positions out of school that don't require a degree. And more than one in five college grads still aren't working a degree-demanding job a decade after leaving school.

My point is that there is a great demand in the workforce. Companies have to pay higher wages in most cases to get higher education. You see, you're sitting in a very good spot, and you won't have all that college debt.

Just for fun, I have listed a few famous people who never went to college or who started but never finished. Trust me, there are many more of them out there, but you get the gist.

- Ted Turner, founder of CNN
- Anthony Robbins, motivational speaker
- Joel Osteen, pastor
- Ray Kroc, McDonald's mogul
- Bill Gates, Microsoft
- Oprah Winfrey, TV host
- Simon Cowell, TV personality
- Tom Hanks, actor
- Matt Damon, actor
- Tom Anderson, founder of MySpace
- Jan Koum, founder of WhatsApp
- Daniel Elk, founder of Spotify
- Mark Zuckerberg, founder of Facebook
- The Wright Brothers, inventor the first airplane
- Steven Spielberg, movie director
- Colonel Sanders, founder of KFC
- Evan Williams, founder of Twitter
- Halle Berry, actress
- Leonardo DiCaprio, actor
- Daniel Radcliffe, actor

Okay, I'm not sure why I added this, but it is cool to see. There is a point here, and that is, you can be successful like these folks without college.

# High School

High school, you either loved it or hated it. You either had friends or didn't. You were either a good student or you struggled. Perhaps you were in varsity or in the school band. Perhaps you were a member of a club. Maybe you were neither of those things because they didn't interest you. Whatever the case, your school did that one thing it was supposed to do, and that was to give you enough information to at least survive. It taught you basic math, English, science, and history. Without these things, it would have been virtually impossible for you to communicate and grow as a person. As awful as you might have thought school was, it was a big part of who you are today. Good or bad, it set a foundation.

That little diploma has more power than you think, my friend. It shows the world that you can learn and you have what it takes to get you there. I know kids who don't have a diploma and the jobs they are qualified for are not the best, I must say. Oh, some might get lucky, but what diploma gives you is an edge over the ones who don't have one when finding a job. Treasure that little paper because you are going to need it later.

I didn't really talk to many people from my school because I had my own issues. I did manage to graduate in the top forty, which wasn't that great because there were only forty kids in my graduating class. Let's just stick with me graduating in the top forty, shall we?

I hated getting up early and sitting in classes all day. I don't miss that, I can tell you. What I do miss was the regiment, getting up early to start another day. I miss the routine because, without it, I became lazy. There wasn't anything there to push me anymore. Without a routine, I would lose my purpose and get very sad, feeling like a failure. You see, guys, you have to have your own purpose. You have to have a reason to get out of bed each and every morning, not sleeping until 2:00 p.m. because you played games all night. Sure, that's fun, but it isn't fair to your parents, and even more, it is truly unfair to you and your future.

Remember, you are the one who is in control of your destiny. Try waking up at the same time every morning for a while until it becomes a routine. Soon you will beat the alarm clock. Stretch a little and ask yourself, "Where am I going and what am I doing today to build my future?" You don't have to be a millionaire and even the CEO of a billion-dollar company. But if you can get a job you really love, one that is more like fun than work, then it isn't work at all. I bet if you were to ask many people if they would give up their high-paying jobs to have a job that they truly loved, you would be surprised by their answer. If you can get you the job you love that pays the bills and allows you some freedom, it is a home run.

I'll bet out of all the teachers you had in school, there was at least one that you really liked, one that made you feel happy to see, one that seemed to care whether or not you came to school. Guess what, there are more of them than you think that really cared about you. I bet that if you needed someone from your high school (no matter if it is the principal, attendance lady, teacher, or even the maintenance person), they would drop everything and help you in a minute. They may have seemed evil when you were in school, but think about how many kids they have that aren't very nice to them.

I know a kid that disliked most of his teachers, but when he needed to study his ASVAB test to get in the military, the principal opened the doors for him to use the school's computers. No matter what you might think, they really do want you to succeed, so keep that little nugget handy in case you ever need it.

# Technical and Vocational Schools

Technical or vocational schools (also called trade schools) are wonderful places to learn a specific trade that you might want to pursue. These fine institutions may be a good way to find your niche and a higher-paying job. Depending on your field of study, it would cost roughly $4,000 to $30,000 for a vocational degree compared to a college, which could cost you $8,000 to $45,000 a year. Also, most vocational schools take ten to eighteen months to complete while a college degree may take four years or more. You can usually find a vocational school relatively close to your home, and most of them simply require you to be sixteen years or older and have a high school diploma or GED.

Here are just some of the jobs you can do with a degree from a trade school:

- Aircraft mechanic
- Carpentry
- Chef
- Computer technician
- Construction manager
- Cosmetologist
- Criminal justice
- Dental hygienist
- Diesel mechanic
- Electrician
- Graphic designer
- Hotel and restaurant management
- Locksmith
- Marine mechanic
- Massage therapist
- Medical transcriptionist
- Motorcycle and automotive repair
- Nursing
- Paralegal
- Pharmacy technician
- Plumber
- Welder

# Certifications

Certifications are awesome. They are relatively cheap and easy to get. The cool thing is that you can do a Google search and find just about any certification you want. Let's say you and three other people have an interview, or better yet, are being considered for a job. If you have a certification, who do you think they are going to choose? That's right. It's you in almost all cases.

You'll find that many certifications can be gotten in as little as two to six months. If the certification is accredited (meaning, recognized), you can even put those letters next to your name on the résumé, which we will get into when we cover résumé writing.

I have always been impressed with someone who takes the time to learn a skill and gain validation from their efforts. This shows future employers that you don't just sit around waiting—you go get it. Things like this can really set you apart from the rest of the field—plus, it gives you more confidence going in. The more certifications, the more you become marketable to a potential employer.

Another interesting thing about certifications is that since you picked it, it won't even seem like school, rather something you really enjoy, so you'll kill it. Once you get your first certification, you will have an "aha" moment and realize you can do anything you put your mind to, and you will become addicted to achieving greater goals.

I like to think of certifications as bragging rights. Just knowing I have all these certifications makes me feel empowered. These are the little things that set you apart from the next person trying to interview for your job.

The confusing thing is, which one do you take? That's easy. Close your eyes and ask yourself, "What do I want to be?" Now open your eyes and find that certification. Keep focused.

Let's get you ready now. I'm confident you will find the resources to get these certifications because people will understand what you are doing and perhaps will help you monetarily. If they know this is something you need to get to the next level, you may see their confidence grow for you.

I still believe that the pure satisfaction of passing and acquiring your first certification is so rewarding that you will be hungry for more. See, you can do it!

# Volunteer

This might be my most important suggestion to you, so take a quick bathroom break if you need it, then come back and pay attention to this, okay?

Now that you're back, let's do this. Volunteering has many advantages—more than you can even fathom. This is single-handedly, probably one of the biggest game-changers in finding a job.

How is that, you ask? Great question. Let's say three people fresh out of high school are interviewing for a job at the same place. Rodney has no other jobs and basically sits in his room playing video games and listening to music. Roy, on the other hand, works two days a week at a clothing store, but beyond that, he does the same thing as Rodney the rest of the week. Then there's Rhonda. She works at some fast-food restaurant place three days a week and volunteers at a hospital four days a week. Who do you think gets the job? Take a guess.

That's right—Rhonda. Why? Because she is the one taking the initiative, the one who is staying busy working toward her future. Rhonda is showing the employer she isn't afraid to work and will work hard.

Another wonderful thing about volunteering is that while you gain excellent on-the-job experience in a working environment, you are contributing to the noble cause of an organization that might not be able to pay someone for that needed help.

My point is that, instead of sitting around, doing nothing, go help someone or something. You'll be amazed at how many people really need your help. There is even a chance through your volunteering that you might just find the job you want.

I know this kid who volunteers two days a week for a hospice care company. His job is to sit with these aging people who are basically at the end of their lives. He just has to keep them company, just listen to them tell stories, and reflect on their lives. And guess what? He loves it. He never thought he would, but three things are happening. First, just by listening to these awesome people and their stories, he is almost angel-like in their eyes. If he had not been there, they would be alone. Second, he is gaining lifelong lessons and worldly knowledge from someone who has truly been there and just wants a little of his time. Third, he is gaining experience. He is performing a job that will help him get a job. Think about it for a minute. A potential employer is interviewing you and asks you how you spend your time when you are not at your part-time job, and you tell him you volunteer for hospice, that you are lucky enough to sit with these beautiful people and hear their stories, and that you keep them company and help them with things they can't physically do. You might see the employer's eyes water up because you, my friend, are awesome.

There are a lot of places needing volunteers. Even if a place doesn't advertise a volunteer need, if you walk in and tell them you are there to help them by volunteering for their cause, they will have a big smile on their faces because people just don't do that anymore.

You know what? You aren't like most people. You are strong with a desire and drive that will set you apart from everyone else. Hey, one of these places may even love the work you do and hire you. I've read that Sean Combs started as a volunteer at a recording studio. Think about that for a minute.

# Self-Employed

Another thing that really shows initiative to an employer is operating your own business until you find a career. You either sit at home waiting for a miracle or go make it happen. This need not be a large corporation with one thousand employees. Keep it small and simple. Remember, you're simply showing your boss you are independent and have a desire to be successful. You know, when I was eight years old, I would pull a wagon all over the neighborhood, looking for pop bottles. Hey, those were five cents apiece, buddy. I would knock on every door and ask if they have any bottles they need to get rid of today. Boy, did I get a lot of doors slammed in my face, but that still did not stop this entrepreneur.

Okay, I'm not telling you to collect empty pop bottles. Just get the idea behind it. You can do many things. You can detail cars for $135 a car. You can cut grass. You can paint people's fences or even their houses inside and out. I know people who walk other people's dogs daily. You'll find people need a relatively cheap handyman who can do odds and ends around their homes. Remember, this isn't your future, just a way to stay busy. This shows initiative and puts a few bucks in your pocket. I know another guy who used to clean windows for people. I also know a girl who gets paid to go to the store to get groceries for older people. You can even babysit. The point to all of this is to condition your mind that the harder you work, the more you will want. That way, if a future job is hard, it won't be a problem for you. Tell them what you used to do. That demands respect right there. As for the girl who would go to the grocery store for people, she never asked her parents for gas or money to go out with her friends. She was usually the one with all the money.

If you think long enough, I'm pretty sure you can think of a job you won't mind doing to gain experience and make a little money. I call it character building. You are building the machine. I think the hardest job I ever did was throwing hay in the summer. Wow, that was hard, especially the day I got stung by fifteen wasps that got bailed up in a hay bail. I'm proud to say I never did that again.

The important thing here is that you show your future boss that you are not afraid of work, that you are a survivor. There are many things you can do. There are jobs that people just don't like to do or are too lazy to do that can make you money.

# Trades

Okay, now I know I said it previously, but this chapter is very important. This is an avenue that can make you lots of money and provide you with excellent benefits and insurance packages that will be extremely important to you down the road. This field is seldom talked about in some schools, and it is virtually never mentioned by your parents. That's right, my new friends. These trades are union positions that are very much in demand and need people just like you. They need highly skilled professionals that start as an apprentice and work themselves into a journeymen, foreman, and superintendent position. You don't need a college degree, and the best thing is that they need you.

While your college friends are at college for four to five years, stacking up huge college debt that will take them years and years to pay off, you are making that money. Many college folks get out of school and, in some cases, get a job that is not even in line with their field of study. But here, you are building a killer future already. By the time they get out of school, you could be a journeyman or higher in the same amount of time it took them to graduate. Plus, it will take them years to catch you in pay even after paying all their loans back. I've even heard some trade folks say that their insurance is better than the president's.

These positions can be found locally (for example, Chicago), and some can require travel in which you work at a project site in a different state until it is finished. The cool thing about that is you can make even more money based on the state's union scale. Plus, you can get a per-diem for the cost of living of $100 a day. That means you can live off that $100 for room and board and still have money left over to eat while leaving your paycheck alone to grow. I know people who buy a camper, take it with them to the project, park it at a campsite, and live there until the project ends.

Now let's just look at what these folks make. We will use Illinois and Indiana as examples, shall we? When you see increases every six months, it is because they take tests to get to the next level. Rates may also vary depending on the location of the project, but I think you get the idea, right? These are just to name a few.

## Pipefitters Local Union 597
Effective 12:01 a.m., June 1, 2019 through May 31, 2020

## Apprentice Rates        Wage Rates
- First year                    $19.40
- Second year                   $27.28
- Third year                    $32.24
- Fourth year                   $38.69
- Fifth year                    $49.60
- Journeyman pipefitters        $49.60
- Foremen                       $52.60
- General foremen               $54.60
- Superintendents               $56.60

## Sprinkler Fitters Local Union 281
All local territory in Illinois and Indiana

- Class I              $22.55 (first 6 months)
-                      $25.10 (second 6 months)
- Class II                      $27.60
- Class III                     $32.60
- Class IV                      $37.60
- Class V                       $42.65
- General foremen               $53.15
- Sprinkler fitter foremen      $52.65
- Journeyman sprinkler fitters  $50.15
- 
- 
-

## Sheet Metal, Air, Rail, Transportation Worker Local 73 Union
Effective June 8, 2019 through May 31, 2020

- Probationary Apprentice     $15.25
- **First Year**
- First 6 months     $17.42
- Second 6 months     $19.60
- **Second Year**
- First 6 months     $21.78
- Second 6 months     $23.96
- **Third Year**
- First 6 months     $27.30
- Second 6 months     $29.58
- **Fourth Year**
- First 6 months     $31.85
- Second 6 months     $34.13
- 

## Plumbing Local 130
Effective June 1, 2019 through May 31.2020

- First 6 months     $17.35
- Second 6 months     $18.85
- Second year     $22.45
- Third year     $25.50
- Fourth year     $33.65
- Fifth year     $38.25
- Journeymen     $51.00
- Foremen     $54.05
- Superintendents     $55.10
-

So with all this being said, how does someone like you become one of these money-making professionals? Well, for starters, you have to be at least eighteen years of age, physically able to do the work, with at least a high school diploma or GED, and a clean criminal record.

You will need to craft a résumé, research potential careers, and enroll in a formal apprenticeship program.

Go to the local Union Hall and ask to sign up for an apprenticeship. Take your résumé and fill out an application. They will most likely give you a test date to come back and take the test. In most cases, how well you do on the test gives you the order for which you will be called. There are practice tests online. Just search on Google.

Another way is to look for companies that already work in the union and apply. You can use job banks by visiting union websites. Research some apprentice programs, and check job boards.

There are also trade non-union jobs in fields like electrician, welding, and fire protection alarm panel building, just to name a few.

The bottom line is that these trades are honest, reputable jobs. They pay great wages and have excellent insurance benefits.

# Résumé Writing

This can be somewhat confusing if you have never had to write this darn thing ever. There are many types, and yes, it is ever-changing. Everyone will tell you that yours is wrong. Look, you will never make every potential employer happy with your résumé style. There are just too many people out there with their own thoughts of what a perfect résumé looks like. Some like to use bold, italics, bullet points, different fonts, and even a certain type of paper. So you won't lose your mind, let's keep it very simple, okay?

Your résumé should flow and read like a menu. It should capture what you do, what you did, and what you want. It is your testimony of where you are from and where you want to go. As you get more experienced and gain additional skills, your résumé can become a little more complex, but for now, let's make it employer friendly.

Some people choose to write a novel about their experience. As an executive talent acquisition leader with over twenty-four years of experience, those types of résumés put me to sleep. You don't need a five-page autobiography. Keep it to one page, two at the most. I prefer a page and a half. I've seen people put their picture on their résumé. I'm not a huge fan of that personally.

There are résumé-writing services available, but that could cost you. At this point, you need to save every penny you have, so let's create one together, shall we?

You must use the correct wording to describe what you do more professionally. Instead of saying that you answer phones, say that you do customer service. You do not put on your résumé that you stock shelves. Instead, you do inventory management. You are not ordering parts. Wrong. You are responsible for purchasing. Are you taking out the garbage? State in your résumé that you have sanitation responsibilities or that you are a recycling coordinator. Do you unload shipments? You can say that you are responsible for shipment allocation. You see, just make it fun, but be truthful. Maybe you are a waitress, but in your résumé, you may say you are a culinary assistant. And you don't do dishes—you are a kitchen attendant.

Just remember to show these potential employers that you are a professional and you are important to their business. So describe your responsibilities like a professional, okay?

## Sample Resume

(Your name here)
(Address)
(Town, state, and zip code)
(Phone)
(Email)

### Profile

(This is a quick summary of your attributes that make up who you are and what you can do for the company, e.g., skills and qualifications. Tailor it to the job you are going after.)

Example: Seeking a full-time position that will utilize my education, communication, organizational, and financial skills to obtain a cashier job.

### Experience

**Hospital**, Valparaiso, IN
2019 to Present
Volunteer
Assist hospital in the emergency room
Responsible for inventory
Customer care associate for patients
Perform customer service duties as required
Partner with urgent care employees
Develop relationships with medical staff

*(Continued next page)*

*(Continued from previous page)*

**Pizza Place**, Portage, IN                    2017–2019
Food Preparation Attendant
- Customer service delivery employee
- Performed duties while in school
- Food preparation
- Inventory management
- Customer service
- Responsible for monetary transactions

**Education**

ABC High School
General Studies
Diploma

(You can leave it to the left like the current job or use bullet points shown on the prior job. It's your choice really.)

(You may also move the employment dates to the right if you like that better.)

# Job Search

Back in the day, people basically had to go to college to get a decent job. This has changed over the years because of the lack of people to fill key roles. You just need to know what it is you want and then map out a plan to go get it. Try to look at finding a job as a game or puzzle. Collect information, keep a log, and work on your presentation skills. It will all come together for you.

Now, this is where you and I need to get a little creative here. There are a lot of places to look for your first real job on the web (I listed some below). However, you must first know how to use them correctly. They not only have a listing of jobs located near you but also serve as a place you may put your résumé for employers to search for you. You will find that most people who are already in the job force don't really put their résumés here because they don't want their current employer to see they are looking for other companies, but for you, it is a great tool to start your career. They pretty much all do the same thing, but the one I like most is LinkedIn. This site not only lists jobs and shows you everything about the company but also identifies who the decision-maker is—hint, hint. You can join LinkedIn and start connecting to people from various companies.

The hardest part about applying directly to jobs online is that there are obstacles you might not overcome. One, in particular, is the number of applications that come in daily. You are up against people from all over, which is why we need to get you ready using the things I mentioned above. Another problem is that if you forget to tailor your résumé and the recruiter doesn't see keywords needed for the job, you are sent to the bad pile. Lastly, a lot of recruiters are overloaded with jobs to fill, and it might take too long before they look at your résumé. That's why you need to build your network and locate that decision-maker so that you can send them your bio personally.

Now some don't like that approach, but it shows one's desire and initiative. Plus, when they receive your résumé, they will typically send it over to the recruiters. The recruiter sometimes assumes the manager knows you, and before you know it, you get a call or, better yet, an interview. Therefore, your résumé needs to be ready and reflect your skills with that of the job you are interested in.

When you use these search engines, input the criteria of the job you want, and let them locate the job for you. It is now your job to bring it all together—the search, the résumé, and the practice for interviewing.

I like to make a strategic game of it. I keep a log of which I have applied with and the status thus far. Keep detailed notes of who you contacted along with their names. Also, when you are on LinkedIn, start connecting to people who work at the company you are interested in. You can use them to get your résumé to the decision-makers. Some people will put more effort into watching TV or playing games than they do at finding a job. That's why I say you have to make it a game. You'll have fun while building an arsenal of potential contacts for future jobs. You will be surprised how fast it is to connect to people, and someday, someone might contact you for help as well.

Another option is a referral after you polish yourself up a little. Don't be afraid to ask a friend or an acquaintance to help you. Remember, if someone gives you a referral, they are telling your future boss that you're a great person and they should give you a try. The worst thing you can do is get hired using a referral and not perform at your best. It makes you look bad and hurts the credentials of the one who referred you, so work your tail off for them.

When you begin applying for jobs, have patience. Not everyone will get back to you in an hour. They are busy as well. Success comes with persistence and dedication. Reach out to several employers at a time, not just one or two. If and when they call you, then be ready. If you miss their call, by all means, call them back, and I don't mean a week later. Show desire and discipline.

Also, when you use other sites to find a job you like, use LinkedIn to find the person in charge and connect with them. Start a conversation and send them your résumé. If you can't find the hiring manager, connect with others in the same company and start from there. You will get the hang of it quickly.

There are many search engines, but these I feel will do great for you. Look at them and get busy, my friend.

- www.Indeed.com
- www.Glassdoor.com
- www.LinkedIn.com
- www.Careerbuilder.com
- www.Monster.com
- www.ZipRecruiter.com

# Finding a Job through Adversities

Now, there are certain negative circumstances beyond our control when it comes to finding a job. One such example is when an economy is in a recession. This is when there is a decline in economic activity typically brought on by a drop in consumer spending. This just means people aren't buying things for whatever reason, so there is a downturn. One recent circumstance is the situation with COVID-19 virus and other previous pandemic outbreaks that have occurred. During this period, many companies are laying people off, terminating, or doing furloughs of their current employees.

So, what does this mean for you trying to find a job? Well, I have always believed that if you do the research, plan head, and polish your persona, meaning get yourself ready, you will conquer all things. You see some people use these situations as excuses, a crutch to not find a job. I hear things from these people like: nobody's hiring; I don't have enough experience or skills; and it's not worth the effort; I'll just wait until the job market comes back.

My suggestion to you is think smart. The healthcare industry needs help, and you don't have to be a doctor or a nurse. There are many positions in the healthcare field that need someone just like you. The greatest thing is that once you get in, you can start developing yourself to advance in your career.

If you were to have a discussion with a few friends, family, or even your high school counselors, and you were to ask which jobs would be needed in the event of a crisis situation, you would discover that there are a lot a jobs that need someone just like you.

The point I'm trying to make is that there will always be the need no matter what the situation brings, and a lot of them don't need a college degree. Here are just a few examples of jobs that appear to be recession proof.

## Recession Proof Jobs

- Medical professionals
- Public Transportation drivers
- Police and Law Enforcement
- Fire Fighters
- Caregivers and social workers
- Hospice Workers
- Grocers
- IT Staff (Computers)
- Librarians
- Maintenance and Repair Workers
- Auto Mechanics
- Sanitation

# Interview Ready

Okay, your résumé looks great. You did the research and found a company you really like that offers a job you really want. You contacted them, and now because you are awesome, they want to meet you in person. Yikes, right? Nah, you got this. Just think positive and act like a professional, and you will be fine.

The date and time are set now. You just have to show up and knock them dead. Before you go to any interview, research the company. Nothing shows more initiative than knowing exactly what that company does and what they need from you. I have seen people lose an opportunity simply because they didn't research the company and, when asked in the interview if they have heard of them, they say, "Not really." Connect with others who work for them as well. This way, not only do you know the company and job description, but you are also connected to people who actually work there. This will ultimately move your candidacy to the top of the pile.

The biggest reason I feel people get nervous in an interview is that they walk in not knowing the people involved or what the company does. If you build relationships with their employees, your nerves will take a back seat to success.

Now, this is important. Never go to an interview dressed like you are going to the beach or to a party with friends. I'm not saying wear a tuxedo, but never wear shorts, flip-flops, a tank top, or a T-shirt. Be better than the other people who are also interviewing for this job. If you don't own a nice shirt with a tie, then wear your best clothes and a nice pair of shoes. If three people show up to the interview in a cardigan and you walk in with a pair of dress slacks, a tie, and a nice pair of shoes, your first impression with the boss will be favorable. Remember, you only get one chance at a first impression, so make it count. Even if everyone at the job site is wearing jeans, you dress slick and show them you mean business. You can wear jeans after you get that job, and make sure you use perfume or cologne so that you smell great.

Another tip is to get some rest the night before your interview. Never walk in with red eyes and yawning because you stayed up all night playing online. You have to be well-rested and quick-witted for the questions they are about to ask you.

Try to show up to the interview at least fifteen minutes early so that you can park and get things ready for the show. I call it a show because you are the main attraction. Put on your best game face and blow them away. Bring at least four to five copies of your résumé in case there are more people in the interview besides the hiring manager. In most cases, you will fill out an application when you arrive, so use your résumé to get the information you need.

When the manager comes to get you, give this person a big smile and a firm handshake because at that moment the show has begun. You are ready, champ. They will ask you questions regarding your résumé or application. Answer in short, to-the-point answers, and whatever you do, don't be a chatty Kathy and just go off blabbing. That is an interview killer. Answer the question they asked. If they need more elaboration, you may talk even more, but you must know when to stop. When they have what they need, they will go to the next question. Tell them what you have done and smile because you are a stud.

They will ask a lot of different questions, such as, "Why do you want this job?" or "Why should they hire you?" Well, you want this job because you did the research on this company and it looks like a wonderful place to work, and they should hire you because you are disciplined, energetic, eager, and ready to start a long career with them. If they ask about money, check the following website: https://www.hrdive.com/news/salary-history-ban-states-list/516662/. The law prohibits many states from asking anything about salary history, so see if your state allows or bans this.

If they can ask this question in your state, then keep it very vague. Let them know you are unfamiliar with their pay structure. Tell them you are more interested in a career with them than pay. Also, let them know that your hard work will overshadow any monetary discussion and that it will take care of itself. Basically, you are telling them "Just pay me what is fair, and I'll work hard to show you I'm worth it." If you blurt out a number that is too high, then more than likely, they may cut the interview short because they can't afford you or you would be making more than someone who has been there for a while.

If they ask for references, give them names of people you can trust will attest to your work ethic. Try not to give them your buddy or a family member. Instead, give them someone who has seen you in action working. It can be a former teacher, a former manager, or a person at the place you volunteer at. These people all make great references.

At this point, they may need a few days to decide, which is not necessarily a bad thing. They might have a few other people they need to consider as well. Then again, they may ask when you can start, and that is a great question. Simply ask them when they would like you to start.

In any event, stand up, shake their hand with a smile, and let them know it has been a pleasure meeting them. However, before you walk out with them, ask one more question. I love this part. I call it the closer. Ask them, "Do you see any drawbacks to me getting this job?" This is a great question because you will catch them off guard, and they will spout out something that might be a reason they won't hire you, and you now have time to close them. Let's say they mention you don't have a car. Well, now is your time to tell them that it is not a problem because your mom will bring you until you get a car or that you only live a few blocks away so getting to work is not a problem. Maybe they wanted someone who has been around food. Tell them that you had home economics in school or where you were volunteering and that you handled food products. In any case, you have a few minutes to make them understand that their concern should not be a concern and that they can trust that you can do it.

At any rate, make it fun. Ask them questions as well. Remember, you are interviewing them as much as they are interviewing you. It takes practice, so do not get discouraged if your first interview goes horribly wrong. Use these techniques I have shown you, and I know you will be successful. Heck, you have a great coach on your side (me) who believes in you, so go get them.

# Confidence

Let's take a deep breath now. I've thrown a lot of stuff at you, so let's take a minute to digest it all. The bottom line is that this is your life and yours alone. You have the chance to be happy and successful, but you must want it. There is no fault here. Maybe you weren't shown how to go get a job, or maybe you weren't quite ready yet. You can only do this for you because you want money, a nice car, or a place of your own. Maybe you want your own freedom. Maybe you like going out to eat or buying clothes whenever you want. Perhaps you simply want to show people you can do anything you put your mind to.

I say we start now with little steps. Never rush into it. You must do the work, and it starts right now. Never think that it's too hard or it isn't fair. That's only because difficulty and fear haven't seen you in action yet. Take some time today and make a goal sheet. Write down the things you want, things you need, and things you want to do.

You know I was once told by my dad that I wasn't going anywhere in life. He said I wasn't as smart as my sisters and brother. I could have just gotten sad and introverted; instead, I used that to feed the beast. The cool thing is that you decide your future. However, you're going to have to leave the baggage behind you, put on your blinders, and look forward. Now go get what is yours.

Hey, look. I don't know you, but I wrote this instructional guide for you because I do care. I've been there, and if what I write helps get your career going, then I've done something great in your life. I think we just need to recondition your mind to think outside the box. You have to think that you are better than a two-days-a-week restaurant job or clothing store job. Think bigger. Think about your career. Above all, do what you love to do so that it will never be work; rather, it will be your passion.

# Conclusion

I have spent over twenty-five years of my life helping people get the job of their dreams and companies get the best-qualified person I can find. I have worked at some of the best technology-driven companies, along with Fortune 100 and 500 companies. I have managed entire teams and implemented recruitment strategies and initiatives.

I find great satisfaction in helping someone go through all the phases of landing that next wonderful opportunity—from assisting them with their résumés to educating them on how to search for a job and become interview ready.

I began feeling like something was missing even with all my success. I'd helped thousands of people but still felt there was this hole.

It finally came to me that it's great to help people already in the workforce, but what about our next generation, the next young man or young lady that just graduated high school? Who is going to help them? I say this with the utmost respect, but this is out of most people's arena. Schools do a wonderful job teaching kids all the education essentials, getting them ready for the world. Parents provide support, which includes food, shelter, travel, loads of their time, money, and love.

There is no blame, but I do feel empathy for all involved. The schools educate, the parents support, and the recipient is tasked with finding a job.

To the parents, you have done a fantastic job. I salute you. However, you can only do so much after the child has graduated. To the schools, hats off to you for providing all the educational tools for them to survive. To the graduates, now what?

Simply put, this instructional book is to help parents nurture their children's growth, assist the schools in educating children and teaching them how to get an excellent job, and lastly, educate the graduates on how to go after their dream jobs.

The decision is now yours to make. Get busy, and make all of us proud, especially yourself.

# About the Author

    **Kevin Johnson** is a husband and father of five boys. He has spent more than two decades helping people find careers and companies find great talent. He is a talent leader, a coach, an educator, and presenter who has changed the lives of thousands of people through employment. Kevin has a deep passion for helping people find their talent and helping them land a job. Your success is truly his reward.
    He is a graduate of Glenville State College in Glenville, West Virginia, and currently resides in Porter County, Indiana.

# Acknowledgments

I have to start by thanking my best friend and wife Nicolette and my sons Jake, Troy, Dillon, Cade, and Lukey. You give me inspiration to be better than the day before.

I'm eternally grateful to Joyce Basel for believing in me and being my biggest critic.

I would like to thank Brent Martinson for encouraging me to keep going. You are a true inspiration, and I admire your compassion for all of your students and staff.

Jason Galoozis, you are a great friend and fellow 219er. Thanks for always being a positive influence, always motivating me to be better.

Trent Albert, you're a great photographer. Thanks for all of the pictures and book support.

Grey Whitney Robinett, I thank you most of all. I am truly the person I am today because of all your support and love. Rest in peace until we meet again my best friend.

www.ingramcontent.com/pod-product-compliance
Lightning Source LLC
Chambersburg PA
CBHW030139100526
44592CB00011B/964